» An Amiable Reception for the Acrobat

»An Amiable Reception for the Acrobat

Poems by Jon Davis

Grid Books BOSTON

GRID BOOKS
Boston, Massachusetts
grid-books.org

Printed by Cushing-Malloy
Ann Arbor, Michigan

ISBN: 978-1-946830-05-0

I heaved myself around literary gatherings like a man with a bullet wound.

Nicanor Parra, "Memories of Youth"

» Night

A fortnight from the cavern, we lingered by the seawall.

What arc, what resonant observation, what delicate

pronouncements by the cookstove? The limber teen

turned cartwheels past the fire. Out of darkness,

briefly mapped by flame-flick and shadow, she romped,

celebrating the fulgent appetites of her kind.

They first discovered it in the sunset, a wash of sudden red that also terri-
fied them. Had something happened in the west? Was this the end? And
then darkness. But the beauty of the stars, the moon like an open mouth
in the sky: they began to see that beauty and terror would travel together.
The shiver of the screech owl in the night. The dove's mournful wail at
dawn. There would be no end. Then snow that made the world beautiful
and desolate. Shimmering, hard. The hawk in its plunder-fall on the prai-
rie; the fox flashing its red and black as it pounced on the mouse, snapping
it beautifully up. Even the bear lumbering after pronghorns—the way he
pulled the straggler down, tore the skin, pushed his face into the beautiful
flesh. And then they looked at each other. Was this beauty, too, these odd
creatures hunkering and wandering, killing and cooking, rooting out food
by the riverbanks?

He is haunted by the past, if by *the past* we mean
just now. The rest is a blur. He wants it that way:

the horses and fevers, the impulsive affairs,
the still pond of gloom he rakes the duckweed from.

Once, he swam deep and long, down where the tadpoles
and turtles lounged. When he rose, a gaggle

of goslings flapped hard and skittered. And the mother
of all that splashing lunged at his long-haired head.

He could have been an otter, could have been
a spaniel, all teeth and pant, all slurp at the belljar.

But here he is, two feet planted in the now.
Big now. Swarmed by duty. Cumulus and cirrus piled

and streaking respectively in the eastern sky. He's up
before everyone and still he's falling behind. Just look

at these kids and their word towers! Who can keep up?
Meanwhile, what Monk's doing between the saxophone's

signature tumult could be played on a toy or a *ragout* of lamb.
Though it'd be less percussive. Though the melodic

properties of lamb are limited to *phfft* and *slosh*.
Like this update, thudded and larded and drizzled

with a muddle of Haldol, of winsome-among-the-larkspurs,
a thin porridge brought steaming in cupped hands

in crisp morning air. An emblem. A forecast. A sign.

» Boarding Groups

A Group

Talk to them, they'll feign an interest;
In all things but seating, they're centrist.

B Group

They suffer fools, mind their manners;
They'll fly, delighted, under any banner.

C Group

They tend to their snacks, shuffle their feet,
Lower their expectations into a middle seat

American Poetry shows up
late, sporting a hoodie & Keds.
Orders a burger. Tosses the bun.

Removes the tomato, the lettuce.
Eats the burger with their fingers,
one greasy chunk at a time.

Their nails are painted green
blue purple red black. W-H-A-T-?
is inked on the back

of their left hand. *W-H-A-T-?*
on the back of their right.
Poetry, it seems, has just one

question. And that is why
this meal is so brief & why
you get stuck with the check.

» The Resistance

When finally he stomped down from the hills and stood,
ten stories tall among the skyscrapers, one vagrant elbow
toppling a small brick warehouse, his wide-mouthed
roar waking the children who hurried to the window,
cupping their hands against the glass to see him better,
we were ready: flame-throwers, rocket-launchers,
tanks and cannons, RPGs assembled on the concourse.
Helicopters circled the colossal head. From their
makeshift post, smug generals surveyed their deployment.
When the firestorm began, when the flames shot skyward,
when the missiles sizzled toward the beast, when the tanks
rumbled, their turrets clicking left and right,
we learned then what we should have always known:
there was no solid beast, no flesh to tear and burn.
Each blast, each flame, each bomb and missile entered
and made him stronger, larger—and worse: the children
in the windows, the iron workers lined along the girders,
the drivers in the stalled and clotted thoroughfares
all began to cheer him on, though he crushed their cars
and swatted buildings down, though he plucked
a light-post, swung it, smashing rows of windows. *Still,*
they thought, *he slogs through blasts and flames as we slog
through our days, beleaguered and heckled and scorned.*

» Of Gwendolyn Brooks

(Golden Shovel)

There
are photos of her smiling; more common is
the downturned mouth, her hand a
puzzlement in the general din. Little
songs scrawled themselves, like lightning
in the air around her head. In
my favorite shot, her eyes look straight through his,
who must have asked the witless question. Her downcast eyes
carry sadness, pity for the unenlightened world. The iron
in that look could clang the bars at
Attica or make her lame inquisitor tremble the
interrogation. It could be she never opened her mouth
that night, could be a look was all she thought it worth. His
thoughts, if there was a *he*, are lost. Her brows
are raised, her lowered glasses ride
her nose, her skin is soft and dark. Neither
the spotlight nor the darkness can own her. Too
steady that gaze, looking past even the far
reaches of this *living*. We're compelled to look up
locked in that now eternal stare. Nor
can we know what churned beneath that cap or down
beneath the jacket, though we hope that nameless *he*
was compelled to drag it clanging through the streets. All we know is
this: when wrongs were rung in language by this poet, she was splendid.

There amidst the smashing glass.
Amongst the tambourined marchers.
Before the door slammed.
Before the drummer stumbled. Before
the scatteration of cymbal and tom,
the crash and rattle of toppling snare.
Before the pharmacist stapled
the bag to the bag to the label
to the receipt. There among
the ordinary gleamings in the silverware
drawer, the wine glass coaxed into song.
Before the ambulances arrived, before
the lumberyard truck started backing
and the geese lay their necks along the grass
emitting the hissing blat we learned
to call honking. Before someone
climbed tabletop and attempted a ragged
Mr. Bojangles imitation.
Before dinner music. Epistemology.
Before the arrival of the latest
tropical depression. Before
Romanticism. Primitivism.
Before the fight song, drinking song,
mystical ravings. Before
baying hounds. Before cartographers
mapped even the darkest caverns
of our collective psyche.
Before blenders. Crock pots.
Before the lap dancer tossed
the man's drink in his face. Before
lap dancers. Before drinks. Even

before faces. Before the hysterical
combatants began shouting for no reason.
Before high-stepping, muscular leaping,
smashing glass, door slams,
stumbling drummers. Before
the cacophonous ceremony
we were beginning to commence to initiate.

Ancillary to what are these intimations of beauty
in the downed jetliner's flotsam, the arched rebuke
of the incoming tide, the single shoe adrift,
butting lightly the creosote pilings? Every takeoff

is an invitation to accident, a clarion to transformation,
if by transformation we mean wreckage, the gone
calling silently back from the insatiable beyond.
We who survive, survive a while only, in grief beside

our styrofoam coffees, the legerdemain of grunt and sigh,
though sometimes in dawn light, a kind of cold beauty
in the sleep-tousled hair, the mouth's O, the childlike
returned to inaugurate the elm's waterfall limbs, to elect

a cabinet of joys—cat perched on the wood plank fence,
daughter smiling anyway among the dandelions and grasshoppers,
the yellow forsythia fountaining by the drought-vexed
wellhouse, the black and orange flash of the beetling oriole.

» Henry at 70. Dawn. Tulum.

Thin & thinner the women here,
& Henry thickens in the heat,
sits zazen in the foam & racket
then strolls down-beach, glances

furtively, drops his trunks &—glancing
off the waves—gallops crookedly into the foam.
In the thicket of his desires
the lovely women roost & preen.

Poor Henry—gimpy rooster in this henhouse—
he carves a thickish cursive when he waddles,
a crooked scrawl that tracks him
like a furtive shadow-self,

its own shady hopes
scrawled in darkness on a tablet
of light. Cursing the infirmities, Henry
gimps shoreward, grapples trunks & sighs.

» Abstract for an Apology

You, who want to parade
your abandonment across every page,

who have made a career of suffering, the intimate
details of that suffering, the indignities and rage,

have left others gasping in the wake of your acts.
And that you have chosen abstraction, the easy

careering among the Latinate, to address the sorrow
you almost feel is, as they say, *telling*, revealing

the gap between your acts and your acknowledgment
that they were, indeed, your acts, that they flowered

not out of the pain you carry like a precious coin
from some distant country, souvenir of a time

when you huddled in a bombed-out farmhouse,
but from the damn-everyone desire of the self-

involved, the man who suddenly
owns the company and cuts the salaries

of those he once worked with shoulder to shoulder
making the armaments he now aims at them.

If this were an actual confession or apology, you would
name the acts: betrayals, abandonments, petty

angers, the times you clenched your fists and shouted
to preserve your happiness only to discover

that what you'd preserved wasn't happiness at all,
but a terrified patrolling of the ramparts,

a long night of scanning the darkness, the friends
approaching, you're sure, with ordnance strapped

to their bodies, smiling, one hand extended in greeting,
the other holding the secret cord.

When he saw it was passing. When he stood in the doorway on an early June morning and really heard the birds—the mockingbird's *chip chip chip chur-ee* in the acacia, the quail pacing and squawking from the parapet, the song sparrow's waterfall trill from its juniper perch. When he watched the clouds pass over and watched new clouds arrive. When he saw the wind in the branches and remembered the bittern he watched swaying with the marsh grass. When images of his young daughter, now grown and living on the coast, began flickering at the edge of thought. When he felt the heaviness in his limbs and felt it passing, his answer was to write it down, to mark its passing by making it more permanent, the way the shale had taken the trilobite his ex-wife had found in Pennsylvania and replaced it grain by grain until there was nothing left of the original creature—only a glittering, intricate mold. Not the trilobite itself, not the creature, but a gathering that marked the trilobite's absence. The way each of his words marked the event, the object, the life that had passed into oblivion, the oblivion of memory which is worn by use, the edges, the glitter, the luster, the sharp definition of each ridge now gone. So that each memory is like the blurred photograph that marks the absence of the object photographed, that is an occasion therefore of speech, of story, so that you hold it up and say, *That black speck was a whale, that blur above him the waterspout.* And it was a cool spring morning and breezy and he held his daughter, she was wearing her white parka, and she wanted to ride the whale, she said, *Could I ride him, could I touch him, could I feed him,* she said. And then the calf appeared alongside the ship breaching and tumbling and clowning and he set her down along the rail and held the back of her coat while she laughed and startled each time the whale rose, until one big eye looked at her and she clapped. It was all passing and she laughed and clapped and looked up at her father, dancing in the center of an almost unbearable joy.

Like brave schoolchildren smiling,
These cottages line the harbor, half joy,
Half fear. The bright colors are all these people know
Of hope, how they coax the sea into giving up

Its seabass, its hake and cod. The skittish sea, ruttish
In winter, when waves the harbor flattens
Pitch boats out past the Skelligs where bright
Fish flash, where Bram O'Connor sees

In gowned rocks the waves festoon, the dress of Mary
At the stable, thick with child, hopeful, but
Fearful, too, like the tale of the eight fishermen, hold
Chock full of cod, who went down in icy seas,

Waves pitching over them, heavy with salt,
Filling their boots, drenching them, chilling them.
Sons of God, they were, and dying, nets strewn on deck,
Hold thick with cod, shouting, they say, Our Fathers

At the end, though nothing could save them
For this cold life. Their bright cottages blurred
Under a salt spray and thickening fog, they
Went down frantic, turned peaceful as the hold

Emptied, the men rising and falling in a bitter sea.
Bright yellow in their slickers, they floated,
Their faces ruddy, grim. Eight men weightless, gone,
Schooling now with those glittering, swirling cod.

» Monk Plays Stride

Outside now, gray sky leaning to rain now,
last leaves clinging, pale green now going paler,
light breeze now twitching, now battering the branches,
while inside Monk is dragging the notes,
behaving himself in homage now, playing
in the dinner jacket now, trying
to play the cracks now between notes now
between beats now, the slur now,
sopping up gravy when no one is looking now,
left leg jitterbugging under the tablecloth,
all the madness stuffed now into that tremor,
all the clowning now, half in now
and half out now of every now game.

» After the Sanguine Election

Good citizens are mostly muscle and ear.
They know the moment but lack
prognostication skills.

They do not anticipate disaster
when they slam the seductive otherworld
in the window's sparkling surface.

Less illusory problems also befuddle
these hearkening machines: Why
year after year the officer shoots

the hoodied teen, and the developer
thrives with his briefcased,
murderous intentions.

A world of menace
and the citizens click and shop—
an obliviousness we would envy

did we not know the consequences.
But citizens have no idea. They tilt
their heads and flee the wind, the shadows

of leaves, their own footsteps.
Stumblebums in the suburbs,
citizens announce their positions equally

to the friendly and the fierce.
They fall asleep in groups, comforted
by the faint contralto of their chatter.

All the fences are electrified; sentries guard every gate. Her position on the divan, while maintained by a complicated system of hoists and gyroscopes, is threatened by the wind pitching over the ridge. And the wind is complicated by the smoke, the smoke by the flames, the flames by the idea of flames that appears suddenly in the book she is reading. Our team of observers asks only that she be provided books in sufficient numbers and of sufficient complexity that they can complete their assessment. You may recall that reader 28 was overcome by a lassitude, an unshakeable angst brought on, it is thought, by the plodding verisimilitude of the texts. Thus the fables. Thus the vorticism. Thus the almost unreadable texts flown in from France and stacked neatly by the divan. That the steady whine and rumble of the trains has proven an occasional distraction, also the tornados bearing down, the howling, the rising floodwaters, the weapons fired during the ridgetop skirmish. Still Reader 29 has proven a fit subject. She reads with a concentration heretofore unknown. Tomorrow we send a team of men in hazmat suits, with revved chainsaws, flame throwers. How is it she turns the page even as the smoke settles around her? And why, when her eyes begin tearing, does she lean ever closer to the poisonous words?

I am happy to speak of your asshole boss,
the curmudgeon who avoided eye contact
at the girl scout cookie booth. Happier still
to discuss your father's aloofness, the nights
he spent reading Proust in the library while you
and your sisters kept cracking the door
hoping he'd glance up and say, *Greta! Lucinda!*
Come in. Let me read you a story about goats
and goatherds, a bell, a bridge, a thatched cottage
and the gray-eyed girls who lived there.

Oh, but you want to talk about how I
was late to the colloquium, poorly coiffed
at your mother's funeral, how I neglected to call
that time I veered, scotch-heavy and bleached
by the Vegas kliegs, into an establishment I know
not the name of, I swear, nor what they were
selling, though whatever it was cost exactly
what I had stashed in my most secret pocket.
Oh, Sheila, my dearest and most tender confidante,
tell me again about that nasty man who peddled

half-frozen corn dogs to the children,
the hairdresser who turned your hair blue,
the cop who stopped you for a cracked
windshield and proceeded to impound the car.
But not about that boyfriend who seemed at first
so *available,* who would talk about anything—

your haughty squash-playing ex-husband,
the angry email, the troubling call—anything,
anything at all except, you now see, his own failings,
and how they made you, of all people, suffer.

» The Failed Spring

Barring a second assault, all should be well.
The current proprietor of the bird house
has launched an encomium of sorts from the acacia
lamenting the previous owner's poorly-made nest
and unhatched eggs, assuring us the new nest,
built directly on the first, entombing thereby
the earlier clutch of speckled eggs, is timed
to coincide with the end of the surprising
cold snap, the unforeseen winds from the east.
That we have chosen to call the group of eggs
a *clutch*. That the brittle remnants
of the oak's leaves, singed by frost, are being replaced
by tiny replicas sprouting like the hands
of the thalidomide boy you once watched
bowling with his feet. And how we love this
chance at recovery, this *overcoming*, this *triumph*
of the spirit, this…what? We know there's a word
for it, or many, in many languages, if we could
only recall them as the fulsomeness regathers
and sweeps over us like a Waikiki wave
or like a memory of other springs. Certainly
these vicissitudes mock our fatuousness, ask us
gently to get down from our high horses.
But whose horses are these? And when did
we mount them? It seems we woke here
already athwart these geldings and mares,
certain that spring would arrive with its lilacs
and birdsong, its vague promise to melt like a bonbon

in the mouth of summer, then disappear
into roguish fall and raffish winter, only to return
with its rains and sudden smells of wet soil,
warblers teetering in the elms, at least so far,
though it is early in this callous
and retributional century.

» "Why don't you finish your manifesto?"

Fernando Pessoa, writing as Henry More

Because I already don't agree with myself.

Because the moon is full and the path that leads to the moon-glanced lake is lined with pine needles.

Because the don'ts are everywhere, like blackbirds flocking over the marsh.

Because capital has already decided everything.

Because the snapping turtle rising slowly from the murky bottom into the green light of the shallows is ghostly in that light.

Because, in the dream, when he sat with the couple, nothing he could say was dispassionate enough.

Because, at 3:30 AM, the trees loom like history and, like history, say *no*.

Because ignorance is full of permission, knowledge rifted with prohibitions.

Because she turned and smiled, undoing centuries of philosophical inquiry.

Because rampant and radical, this world.

Because the finch fidgeting in the hemlock, the coachwhip slipping through the bird-loud courtyard.

Because *Manifesto* is a thin mountain stream, and I want the glacial lake
    in moonlight.

And all the springs and rills and rivulets emptying into it.

» Memorandum: Inputting Outcomes Assessments for Individuals
   Currently Enrolled as Post-Secondary Arts Education Consumers:
   A Report Composed by the Consulting Group Upon Completion of
   the Recent Site Visit

Because the flatulent professors
remain deadlocked. Because
they are plagued by memories
and unremediated squalor.
Because in each cubicle
hangs a photograph of the insipid
paying homage to the inane. Because
the Encyclopedia of Unstable Referents
has been consulted. Because the armature
is spinning without effect
or noticeable profit. Because
the students have lost their purchase
on the cambered slopes of *laissez faire*.
Because the night sky has been instructed
and authorized. Because we have been
unable to assess. Because someone sang C
when we pointed to D. Because the overhead
transparencies, the computer printouts.
Because these numbers, when plotted
against the national average, do not exemplify
the enhanced outcomes we'd predicted
during our previous visit. Because
these brush strokes
fall outside the parameters. Because
the message is unmeasurable and is plagued
by interference. Because
the signifiers seem randomly placed.
Because such phrases as

"April is the cruelest month"
present undecidable propositions.
Because your students' works escape
the tools we've designed to capture our data
and, therefore, do not, strictly speaking,
exist. Because we are not authorized
to modify the apparatus. Because our studies
clearly demonstrate an accuracy
plus or minus three percent.
Because we are dedicated
to indexing measurable
arts-related activities,
we regret to inform you
that we can no longer validate
your institutional outcomes.

» After Conducting a Thorough But Preliminary Investigation
We Have Come to Some Tentative Conclusions Regarding the
Allegations of Abuse Lodged by the Defendant

Let me get right to the point: Mistakes were, apparently, made. We'll be
the first to admit it. The perpetrator should not have been handled with
such alleged force. The alleged weapons should not have been wielded
with such alleged force. The perpetrator's head should not have been
allegedly struck with such force. His alleged arm should not have been
wrenched (albeit allegedly) back. The alleged stun guns should not have
been employed. We regret also the allegations regarding the use of ropes
and nets. These allegations will be addressed in the afternoon press confer-
ence. The perpetrator's girlfriend, hereafter the perpetratoress, should not
have been allegedly handcuffed to the car door handle and subsequently
struck, allegedly and repeatedly, with a blunt instrument. Am I making
myself perfectly clear? Mistakes were made throughout the operation.
The perpetratoress's purse should not have been allegedly spilled onto
the pavement. We regret such alleged actions. She should not have been
hand-searched by the male officer, as alleged. Certain regions of her alleged
body should not have been lingered over by the alleged officer. She should
not have been allowed to knee said officer in the groin, a crime for which
she has been charged. We regret these errors though, unfortunately, we
cannot accept responsibility. This was a difficult case. These officers work
in a climate of fear and distrust. Frames 40-45 of the videotape show this
clearly. Whether you see smiles or grimaces on the officers' faces will be
the subject of a forthcoming report. We now believe the officers' shouts
of "Shock the Monkey" refer to a currently popular rock song and not to
the ethnic makeup of the suspect. Please be assured that no detail will
go unexplained. All of these mistakes were, given the climate of fear and
distrust, unavoidable. As for our critics, we would only ask them to ask
themselves, Have *you* never made a mistake? A complete investigation
will be conducted; however, we are only human and fully expect these
mistakes to continue unchecked.

» When Stevie Ray Plugs In

for Greg Glazner

A little twitching among the tubes.
A radiance in the diodes. A few
quick words about love & cash.
Shine a light over here, the notes say.
Shine a light on this happening down
here among the wrenches & rags.
Could you hold that still, they say.
There's something down in the dark—
wet & slick. Something down there,
burdened by all the touching.
Could you could you could you.
A long silence, a single note
shaking in the heart's vault, the brain
saying *what.* Saying *could you share
those blankets.* Then it's momentous
& good: Cat scratching the sofa arm,
dog rolling onto its back, sunlight
wrapping its golden arms around
everything—splayed books, flowers, vine
slinking through the vestibule, plane tickets
in their sliced folders. Then a staggering
and lurching, a howl, another howl,
something stirred up in the muddy shallows.
Bees in a box. Sirens
and a steady hand. A choir of nerves.
Here inside the aftersprawl
of the incendiary of the hard choice.
Look: A long amber thread. A sweet
miracle, shimmering & shivering
in sunlight. Someone has drawn
the spoon out the honeyjar.

» Blue Monk

nobody knows where the music is taking us
the head anchors us against chaos
the piano's contradictions pithy asides
the sax growls then turns sweet then
dips down to chide the rhythm section
the drummer *dropping bombs* or skipping
jaunty and joyful the piano gone Monk
sips a drink or just waits his eyes
closed dreaming or scheming a way
in without a plan save slipping
from this chord to the next surfacing
like a river otter *here there here*
diminishments and augmentations leaving
thick tracks then scuffling lightfooted over
wet ground high hat and the bass's querulous
solo outraged Monk bursts back into the moment

» Peat

at Cill Rialaig, County Kerry

A low flame brings back memories
of bog light at dawn, her first love.
That old flame will cool her to the new.
So prepare a hot fire. Surprise her.
She'll forget about the bog.
She's been intimate with wet
and cold so long she wants to burn.
But don't leave her alone too long;
she'll dream herself back
to that boggy grave. Blow lightly
on her neck. She'll flare anew.
Remember: this is a quiet date, not
a prelude to a party. Huddle
close with a glass, a cup of tea.
She'll love to gossip and whisper—
a pensive ticking in the stillness,
a thin humming under wind.
She'll love attention, but not
the heroic gesture. Just a light touch,
a gentle shifting on the bed.
One small mistake, one touch
too heavy, one ill-considered
phrase, and she'll shut down,
go moody, dark. But if you're good—
and lucky—she'll catch slow, burn hot.
A widow finding new love, she'll
laugh and shake her red hair loose.

When did you first notice the change?

Whales were breaching off the coast of Utqiaġvik; scientists were
    sketching fluke patterns.

What evidence led to your conclusions?

Dogs lunging, in winter and in North Dakota, at the pregnant protester.

Do you have a plan to avert catastrophe?

The presidential candidate shouted "Beat them up!" shouted "Toss
    them the hell out of here!"

Is there any hope?

A hummingbird perched, red-throated, among the reddening leaves of
    a sumac.

Is it already too late then?

Clouds of purple and yellow asters line Rabbit Road.

Can you tell us what it feels like to know what you know?

A woman with sticks lifting raffia cloth from the dye-pot.

What can we expect next?

The lamb, still wet from birth, legs shaking, nudging and butting the
    mother's cold flank.

Nobody was happy with the apocalypse. For some it lacked drama. Many had hoped for a series of explosions, bands of bulked-up, tattooed men riding atop mongrel machinery, hair blowing in the apocalyptic wind. Others hoped for lost tribes scrabbling across the windswept ghost cities, battling with remnant weapons for the small caches of unspoiled food that remained. Still others had hoped for clashes between superpowers featuring Blackhawks and stealth bombers, lasers fired from remote-controlled satellites. For some, the lack of a moral proved disturbing. Where was the righteousness we'd expected? Why hadn't the virtuous been sorted from the sinful? Where was the complex system of rewards and punishments we'd embraced? The randomness of the apocalypse was a topic that confounded many of the apocalypticians. Nobody had foreseen the long, slow, boring demise. Entropy and ennui, it seems, had few supporters. Nobody had predicted that the apocalypse would be marked by resignation and waiting, that the apocalypse would be more of a terminal diagnosis than a series of heroic interventions. Of course, there was drama when we understood it was over. When the measurements were taken. When the scientists appeared alongside the presidents and prime ministers and religious leaders. When they made the grim pronouncement. When the game was called because of darkness. Many of us gathered briefly in the streets to take action, but no action could be agreed upon. The wealthy and powerful had caches of food and drinking water. We knew they'd outlive us by days, months, maybe years, but most agreed this was no advantage. The scientists had run out of tricks. The food supply was dwindling. There was no clean water. The shift to solar energy made for an unending source of power, especially as the ozone layer thinned and disappeared, so most decided to go inside and play video games or watch television and movies, search the web for music videos or videos of someone doing something incredibly stupid on a skateboard. Facebook became painful as lethargy and death made for a scroll of loss. Messages from afteriamgone.com started being forwarded in huge numbers. Letters from the dead pouring into the mailboxes of the living. Occasionally gunfire would erupt on the streets and people would mute their televisions and listen wistfully until the gunfire ceased. When the end came, we lifted our heads and nodded. The computers and videos went on without us, the animated characters dying and restarting, dying and restarting, the jingles floating out over the otherwise silent streets.

» Henry at 70. His Skittish Rut.

The wick at both ends hissed then hushed.
And *could* made Henry throng
some sultry Henrietta.
Oh, hid & huffed did Henry then.

"Hideous this life!" he cried,
to float such *sultry*
starboard of his harboring skiff.
His wicked histrionics, muted

to a mewling wicked through plaster
were emblem of his skittish rut,
a *wouldliness* without the *can,*
a wild cry

in a wilderness of flesh.
A canny cry, not mute entire
but aged into a skittery clutching,
ear cupped to her faintly mewling heart.

The hands that carved the stones are gone,
Took love with them to their graves. Not love,
Exactly—care of man for man—but the pleasure
Of a line well-carved, an Irish rune, some
Filigree, a rose, a Celtic cross cold chiseled
Out of stone. Against wave and wind.
Against dusk and dawn and dusk again.

The Skelligs drift seaward in their rocky ships.
First Michael, then the other, lesser one.
Home to puffins with their Botticellian beaks
And ghosts of monks so relic they left
Hardscrabble behind to sail, to cut six hundred
Steps, set stone on stone, where even water
And bread sang out like sirens from the rocks.

Graves are gaudy now on Skellig Loop,
Cut by machines no man's hand guides. You pick
Your icons from a catalog, stones on-line.
Two men from Cork come stumbling with a map.
But the Abbey graves set sail still at dawn
Into wind-lashed waves that wash the graves
Of fishermen. The wives, who stayed behind,

Now, under pitted Celtic crosses, sail, snug
In their husbands' arms for the cold crossing.

» The Campaign Manager Talks Shop

The man was no one till I made him up.
A stork of a man in green and plaid. I calmed
The North Sea of his haberdashery
And taught him not to blink.

He was so partisan, he'd insult an aunt
At tea before he'd compromise himself.
He'd stumbled through two local votes
On buffoonery and tactlessness—the townies

Thought him "frank." But the TV's eye
Made him look half Harpo Marx, half
Richard Speck. The warmth the locals felt
In his handshake and dishevelment

Was dampened in the kliegs. His frankness
Turned to vacancy; his small town
Turned to hick. Even his young wife,
Professional and caring, fled the screen,

Got my name from friends of friends.
Next day at lunch, I scoped him out.
He was genuine, all right. Just wanted
To help out. Old fashioned, simple,

Honest. We'd have to beat that out of him,
Convince the voters he was simple-sly.
I had him measured for blues
Before dessert. Red striped tie, black shoes.

I'm a seer not a manager, and the vision
That unfolded as we ate and chatted
Was projected by the room—the voters
Poking at their salads, swirling wine.

A candidate is half illusory, half solid.
The former is my business. Over coffee, he poked
A finger gently in the air—JFK, I thought,
And made a mental note. His voice was shrill,

But we could soften that. His hair, untamed,
Recalled McGovern's unkempt mop—too liberal,
Cerebral, indecisive. I'd have it trimmed and sprayed.
Some shyness leaned him forward, made

His shoulders round. "Eye the camera
Like a friend," I told him. "Step *to* the crowd
And let your voice go soft." The women
Like a boyish tone. The step? Pure Kennedy—

Something for the men. His bulbous nose
We'd have to live with. I'd hire a boy
To watch for glare, aim a fill light at
The shadows that made his nose

Look comical or mean. It undercut
The smartness in his eyes, the eloquence
That gathered 'round his mouth.
I'd feed him vitamins, keep him healthy—

One cold in that clown-schnozz
And the campaign comes crashing down.
After lunch, I shook his hand. It was,
As all reported, hearty, warm.

He was genuine, all right. I spent a week
Laying out a plan. I brought it to him—
A slick, impeccable assault. It couldn't miss.
He turned me down. Said it wasn't image

That he wanted. He insisted on being
Something he called "real." I signed on
With his opponent. We trounced him at the polls.
I saw him in the grocery next day.

He smiled, shook my hand. He seemed
Completely happy to have lost.
I was right, he said, about the suit,
The tie, the lights. But about the nose,

He said, I'd gone too far. "I may
Seem half-buffoon and goofy bluster,
This far from homelessness and drink.
But failure, or the look of it,

Keeps me humble, real. I'd rather lose
Than lose myself." He yanked a cart
From out the stack; I yanked one, too.
I liked the man, his principled

Foolishness, and followed him awhile
As he drifted down the aisles, almost aimless,
Sniffing melons, sorting through the breads,
As scanners beeped and checkers hustled

And a muted, comforting music filtered
Down through thick fluorescent air
On all of us—Americans,
Wheeling through the commerce of our days.

Time in the Russian sage, tangled there, implicate in the bright blossoms. But what is time for the hummingbird? Here then there. No *then*. Here. There. Here again. But no *again*. Not exactly. Here. There. Here. No exposition. No narrative summary. No flashbacks. No past. No future. Here. Now. On the radio yesterday a woman explaining how the spleen distributes the sourness, the sweetness to the necessary organs. But the biology, the evidence, won't sustain that theory. That *poetry*. Unless a theory of *charm*. But how to articulate that. The words are digital, and we want the flow of time, the sweetness in the flower of time. The hummingbird distributing that sweetness as joy, coppery for no reason, sliding impossibly forward then back, an entire creature no bigger than your thumb.

Once on the edge of a bay, they watched the laughing gulls gather at
 dusk, falling out of the sky like quick, sharp memories of shame—

In the swarming red of sunset the gulls all turned to face the sea—

Was it bounty or terror they awaited?

The symbolism was painful, if somewhat obtuse—

The black and red of the pileated woodpecker in the ghostly green was
 either beauty or doom—

They could hear the claws catch bark, the *kuk-kuk-kuk-kuk-kuk* just as
 the field guide had predicted—

The fear was inside but it was easy to project it into the swamp—

What's that in the grass? she said—

The chances were the same each time but that was not the way it felt—

The world was an augur a proboscis an ovipositor a vector a fang—

That they eventually drifted apart had little to do with them—

What seemed to be a log was an alligator—

What sounded like teenagers splashing in the surf at midnight was,
 the experts told them the next morning, the thrashing of crocodiles
 cruising the shallows to feed—

First frost and the woodstove ticks and sighs.
Yesterday, walking out, I spooked
two meadowlarks. Spooked them again
on the walk back home. The whole day
around them grayed and brightened,
turned sooty again. But they had not
a single good idea of what to do. Like us, then.
New wives, new homes. Same old song.
Like a creaking gate or something electronic
wired briefly wrong before the breaker snaps.
The frost here gleams silver until ten
on the northside slopes. Stoking the woodstove,
I heard that old song crank up in my head—
Augie on the roller-rink Farfisa, Sir Doug
pleading, *Please stay here with me*
in Mendocino. Nothing to it but pine and sigh,
yet there it was, honking in my brain. Same post.
Same song. Same flash of yellow when they fly.
This morning, hurricane toast on the hot plate.
Coffee from a bag, not the stoic cowboy kind.
And radio all the way from Boston on the laptop.
The tempo's shifted since '84. My new book's
a page turner, but not how you think. Imagine
a man rummaging for a matched pair of socks
and you'll have it. I've been that man.
And I've been the man stooped beside a cabin
near Bear Creek in the thirty-degree morning
tapping a poem onto an iPhone. This poem.
You're right to say that's wrong. Imagine Keats
on an iPhone, chasing the Wi-Fi down
among dogs and cows in a frosty pasture.

Had he lived now, he'd have made 85
and we'd all be sunk. Rob, yesterday a coyote
bounced across the road, tongue hanging,
and slipped into the dark draw below me.
Rumor has it they don't feel joy. But maybe
the joy was all mine. Maybe Rilke was wrong,
and we're not here to *name* things but to *feel* them.
In that case, looking isn't a prelude
to anything, this glass of Laphroaig neither
inspiration nor celebration. Cheers, old friend.
If I see the dust billow in your headlights,
hear the clatter of loose tappets, I'll get the gate.

» Still Life with Tarnished Spoon

> "I made the wrong mistakes."
> THELONIOUS MONK

I. A CHAMPAGNE GLASS

Times when you could feel the snapshot congealing around you.

Light a fifties light. Colors artificially bright.

The day M slammed J's finger in the car door.

The faded sunstruck blue of the car.

White crease. Line of blood. Finger dangling at the joint.

Single mother at the wheel, aunt yanking the door open.

Grandmother, widowed, arthritic, hovering behind lace curtains.

Screaming children unloaded.

Car graveling hard toward pavement.

Surfaces scrubbed. The run, chromatic.

Landing on the tonic so everything was settled.

But all that gorgeous damage along the way.

Finger backed with metal, gauze-wrapped.

Mummified finger. Trophy. Key.

He had *cystic fibrosis*.

It sounded like something a priest might chant.

Boxes filled with jars full of pig enzymes in the bathroom closet.

Best known for his farts. Baby face.

Impish smile in the heave and heft of his odors.

Later, his bowling.

Stork-thin, he swung the 16-pound ball toward the hardwood.

Set it there like a champagne glass.

II. Shaft

"Working with Monk'" John Coltrane said, "is like falling down a dark
    elevator shaft."

This dark, for example. This shaft.

The day the cheerleaders spread across the lawn, shouting in their
    husky voices.

Boys on their knees in the upstairs window, watching. A little terrified.

The break here: Jaunty. Whimsical. If it had words, they might be:

> *I HEAR / someone like you / talking through the wind chimes.*
> *I HEAR / voices in the stovepipe / sighing in the air ducts.*

The raccoon family had wandered through the neighborhood in
    the night.

In the morning a single baby raccoon, stranded under the playhouse.

Not yet weaned, it sucked our fingers, licked our necks.

Put its cool hands into our ears.

How could we not. We did.

Once launched himself onto the Avon lady's leg, threw his own legs
    around one of hers.

Hugged her hard while she hooted and tried to shake him off.

When we finally released him, he went straight into our house.

We drove him across town.

Two days later, he hopped up the steps to our back door.

We drove him to the next town, watched the fence line for days afterward.

III. Happening

"You can't make anything go anywhere," Monk said. "It just happens."

Happening in the sunset over the frozen marsh.

Happening in the harrier's looping flight over the cattails.

Happening in the crenelated blow-worm writhing in the rabbit's throat.

IV. Mistakes

Were these the right mistakes?

The father drove the D-10 dozer into the drainage pond.

Left it running there. Swam ashore.

The right mistake?

The father berated the boy for dressing like a girl on Halloween.

The right mistake?

Late night fire in the vacant lot.

The right mistake?

Wife and children packing and leaving while he was drinking at Harry's.

The right mistake?

Hiding the children with relatives on the backroad farm.

Not quite family. Not quite strangers.

The right mistake?

Younger brother staring at the road, at the disappearing car.

The right mistake?

V. Family

It wasn't a family that talked much. It was a family of elisions.

Surplice and *dowager*. *Divertissement* and *succubus*. *Stumble* and *decree*.

Long silences at the breakfast table.

Yellow flash of flicker wings on the neighbor's mossy lawn.

Orioles in the fountaining willow.

Sugar in the sugar bowl, tea-stained and clumped by the tarnished spoon.

» The Rebel Makes His Stand Before Leaving

This town of dust and food-smeared
kids can't hold me. At school
they toss a loop of rope around your neck
and pull it tight. They tie an arm and both
your legs and leave you sprawled like that.
Here's what they offer in exchange
for freeing both your arms: A place to stand
between two other dying men who pull
the same red lever on the same machine;
a house with a view of another house
with a view of another house with a view;
an acre of grass and enough technology
to wreck your Saturdays; a closetful
of rods and reels, three days a year
to drift your flies past unappeasable trout.
I'm getting out. This van's white eyes
already stare beyond the darkness
of the Interstate. The engine ticks
and hisses, and dreams of places West—
L.A., 'Frisco, Hollywood. I'll hang
my Strat waist high and slide this
bottleneck along the twelve frets
of my future, then slide it back again
until the whole town shatters and falls
like glass around me. I'll play the Yellowstone's
dull plod, our parents' furtive slap
and suck, the spoiled daughters,
chosen sons, the thump and squeak of basketball,
the clack of shoulder pads and helmets.
I'll play the mines and pastures that keep
calling us from the radio's ten songs,

the old folks in their tube-steel cages
scuffling past the Handi-Stop, the values
of the FFA—work and wear your cap
and kiss the flag and die. My van
is sleek and ready and a different music
rocks it like a beast that's caged
too long. I know what they say—
I'll wind up in a ditch. And you?

Born tumbledown and fleeced. Born unregulated, toxic from the start. Tricycling into the matte dawn of Myddletown, the heaped and grassed, the concrete walkways, the symmetrical shrubbery and zinnias, the gas guzzlers braked and ticking. Dusty blinds scissored open and peered through. More package store than library. More deli than sitdown meal. More bag of sandwishes. More wash-up and come to table. Meat, potatoes, green beans. Spaghetti, meatballs. Burgers on the charcoal grill. Casserole and milk. Into this, hands-raised and dancing to the tinny Elvis-inflected radio, hurling himself at the wallpaper, eating with his hands, slurping when he drinks, comes little Charles, Charlie, Chuck. What's he into now, that cantankerous, splendiferous child? Gone off to the woods again? Following the sapsucker from yard to yard? Splashing in the pubbles? Reading above his weight, punching at another grade level. Brawling with the puppy. What next, Chuck. What next? Books books books. Fevered in the wordrow. *Spiderman* and "Self Reliance." Space travel and alien encounters and Paricutin, breathing ash in the cornfield, "red flames of fire rising into the darkened sky that burst like golden marigolds, while a rain like artificial fire fell." You could hope for such beautiful devastation or make it up, thought Chuck as he Zorroed through the woods with his willow-branch sabre. As everything Paricutined around him, birds whistling and crying, newts floating in the drainage ditch, turtles scuffling in the blackberry fields. And so he was launched, a pitch-pocket roaring blue-hot.

» Leadbelly

for Chuck Calabreze

Because the two women in the Rathskeller,
at the stageside table, were stirring
their rum & cokes absently, ignoring
the strident folksinger, & because one
kept tucking a stray strand of hair
behind a perfect ear, pierced, with a silver
earring shaped like a tear hanging
from it, I nearly stumbled over the tattooed
biker who was collecting admission.
My muttered apologies were like
the tentative mewlings of a kitten
finding itself scratching for the first time
at the back door's cold side.
Not even God, whom we must hold
responsible for the hair & the ear,
for the oddly distracted way she poked
at the ice in her drink, could explain the shiver
or whatever it was that shinnied up
my spine & rapped at the base
of my brain until some memory
laid itself like a transparency
over the whole nightclub. Okay, forget God.
Forget explanation. There was no club,
no strident folksinger, no earring shaped
like a tear. Instead, there is this:
When I was eleven I thought girls
were some rare, previously undiscovered
species rescued from extinction
in a rainforest somewhere, hauled back
to baffle me with their inexplicable customs.

Like saying forever when they mean
pass the remote. Okay, I confess: I
invented the club & the women
for the sake of this poem. Hoping
they might lift me, like a diseased organ,
out of the anaesthetized body of my days.
Hoping they might keep me from saying things
like the "anaesthetized body of my days,"
which sounds like bad T. S. Eliot.
Poor Tom, who never learned the hully-gully
or heard The Replacements sing "Alex Chilton."
Meanwhile, I've become the ragged,
bearded man wearing a half-dozen
sweaters scavenged from the Goodwill
shack in the K-Mart parking lot,
only I'm holding up a different hand-lettered sign:
"WILL WRITE FOR SYMPATHY,
ATTENTION, FOR A CHANCE
TO TOUCH THAT WOMAN'S EAR."
Which is what I'd rather be doing.
The thought of that woman is like
the coffee grinder crunching then
whirring that night I slept in the spare room
next to my best friend's kitchen
while he & his wife took turns
arriving at their amicable divorce
by crashing plates against the hardwood floor.
After seeing Marshall Crenshaw
at the Paradise. After listening to him sing
"Cynical Girl," hearing him find that place
where grandeur meets the mundane
in the high-pitched keening. After
the leaf-scattering ride home in my friend's
Camry. After coffee. After the dishes

and Leonard Cohen croaking "Everybody
Knows." Everything unravelling. The future
unknown. Like stewed prunes. Like
some new color sprouting in the bread drawer.
My uncle said we'd find acid
at the center, but there was only
a tiny rubber ball. In the dream, a woman
in a gorilla suit, her gorilla-hair coiffed
in that Farrah Fawcett flip from the American
seventies, kept whispering, "I want
to have your baby," and I kept replying
with a Shakespearean flourish, "I'm sorry,
but I shan't be siring a child, Ma'am."
And then there were all those baguettes
in the sunny marketplace—such plenty
& sadness like a sliver you realize too late
you should have tweezered out right away
& the redness surrounding it like the
afterglow of "making love" with a woman
you know you will never see again.
Snail darter. Kirtland's warbler.
Greater Auk. Dodo. Gone or going.
I'm sorry, it's just that when we
placed the pellets on the stove burner
what squirmed upward looked
nothing like snakes & how do you
explain that to your younger brothers,
gathered stoveside to witness
your mastery? I swear those snakes
were like gray, crusted toothpaste
squeezed from the tube. Watching them curl,
I understood that I was becoming
the sort of man who would say ramshackle
at a bus stop, cartilaginous

in mixed company. The women
at the Rat would have liked those snakes;
they would have poked at them
with their tiny, impractical straws.
So much liquid through
a one-millimeter opening. Volume
over Time et cetera. Did I mention
the gorilla suit? On stage,
the folksinger-who'd-once-met-Leadbelly
stomped & howled. Like a wise man,
Leadbelly was; like a boddhisatva but
drunk, he said. And he stomped &
howled some more. Stomped & howled
like it meant something. And then,
flush with all that meaning, he packed up
his battered Gibson & hobbled
through the glass doors & on up
Boylston, straight out of this poem.
Sunburst, they call it, an adjective
that furrows my brow with worry.

I have sent my supplications into the night and the emptiness has answered me. The stars still wear their same fragrant socks. The moon has kicked its boots off and harumphed. The trees are tired of your ministrations. All night you whistled through the half-shut window. I am taking this up from now on with the district manager. She says you have certain responsibilities, many of which you have failed to meet. For example: The worms on the rain-soaked boulevard, the horses rolling by the water hole. That you have not scattered the trash uniformly along the interstate. That you have underwritten the havoc in the playroom and have not cited the swallows for their incessant skittering over Ellison's Pond. All the citronella candles winked out at midnight without a single empathetic moan from your minions. That no further mendicants have been spotted along the wagon trail is probably a sign you should take seriously. Have you thought of the implications of your incessant thrashing of the lilacs? Authorities higher up than you have indicated that you will be cited. It's true no jail can hold you, but other punishments are being suggested. The ball and chain, the highway work crew. Public humiliation. A pink cap and a T-shirt carrying a list of your crimes. How to properly punish you is the subject of an upcoming symposium. You, of course, are invited to attend. Some have suggested bigger trees; others have suggested a long, flat prairie. Myself, I have tried to empathize. I have tried to see how you might be reformed. Some say these mischievous impulses of yours arise naturally, as you drift across tropical seas or swoop down over our dreary deserts. The yachts of disappointment, some say, hold their stupid regatta in your heart. They say you are incorrigible. Unrepentant as a cow on a highway. I am trying not to believe that's true. If you would meet me at midnight outside the new Explosion Factory, I would intercede on your behalf. I believe you are misunderstood. I think I can show that your intentions are good. I will never forget the blow worm in the rabbit's throat, how you flushed that rabbit from beneath the swamp roses so that my younger brother might slingshot him to death in the clearing. Nor will I forget how you caused such great suffering that autumn when trees fell on houses and water rushed into the basements and electrical wires sparked along the suburban thoroughfares. When order was restored the sun never shone more brightly.

Your friend and loyal supporter (so far),

Bucky Sherman

P.S. I was at the Slurpee machine when that school bus swerved to miss the toppling crane and crashed into the 7-11. I don't blame you for my deafness, and I am grateful for the paralysis which has made the loss of my legs less tragic; however, I do wish you could find time to visit me here in the home.

These new covenants are baffling. The recently erected "Skyhook" monument was intended as a paean to your great works, not, as you interpreted it, a critique of the lack of worldly justice. As you wished, we have dismantled it and put the bland "Future of Commerce" monument in its place. The white motif has been carried to its final extreme, however, and we all look forward to the loosening of current restrictions. Though we cannot comprehend your insecurities and sneezing fits, many of us continue to speak well of you. In your honor, The Artisans Guild had scheduled a mime performance for next Wednesday at noon in the Marketplace. Now that we have received your recent "Covenant Regarding the Use of Face Paint," they have been forced to schedule a hammered dulcimer concert in its place. Your much-admired "Covenant on the Behavior of the Lame in Public Places" was roundly applauded; yet, even here, some have questions about your "biases." Certainly, the sight of my paralyzed form created a stir in the Marketplace, but then so has the prescribed wearing of "The Caul of the Gimpy." We all agree there is a problem; a few dispute the effectiveness of the solution. We continue to peruse your documents and have appointed a "Commission on Explication." Their work has been constrained, however, by what might, were it the work of some other agent, be called harassment. The ball of fire which began burning in Abigail Porter's chest when she criticized the wording of the "Covenant on Neighborly Behavior" seems, in retrospect, excessive. Some on the commission have questioned your self-esteem. True, the questioning ceased when their cars began exploding in the parking lot, but I think they may have had a valid criticism. Our local artisans continue to replicate the items in your sacred haberdashery. And we are pleased to honor you by dressing as you prescribed in your "Covenant on the Wearing of Gold Chains and Platform Shoes." But, again, there have been some rumblings of, shall we say, discontent regarding these prescriptions and codicils. Some would like to relax in khaki and old sweatshirts; others would be content if they were allowed to wear—how shall I put this—less colorful platform shoes. The

"Covenant on the Sacred Arts of Podiatry and Chiropracty" has helped some to lead healthy, vigorous lives, but others, many others, have had to begin wearing "The Caul of the Gimpy." As spokesperson for the commission and the community, I would be remiss if I did not mention the lukewarm response to the most emphatic of your recent covenants, the "Covenant Regarding Heedless Spending." While we also believe that thrift is important, we would like to believe that spending money to "feed a squalling child" is not "heedless." Even the most content children will, on occasion, squall. We would like to think that a single episode of squalling could be overlooked. Still, you no doubt have a point. As spokesperson for the commission, I have been asked to bring these issues to your attention. I will remind you that I am already paralyzed and operate this computer by blinking as a row of letters races past. Perhaps that is why the commission chose me. Yet, I'm not alone in my fear that you will soon be gracing us with a "Covenant Regarding Excessive Eye Movement." Given your omniscience, you will have already received this letter long before I wrote it. Please keep these limits on my free will in mind as you deliberate on my punishment.

Your Humble (but ever so slightly jaded) Supporter,

Bucky Sherman

» Maturity

If in the hours of digital clocks flashing, the
hours when the neighbors' dogs haggle over
who pissed on this hydrant, on that utility pole, the hours
called in the modern discursive formation "lonely,"
the woman you're living with sits upright, still
asleep, and begins patting the mattress like
she's lost something, what should you do?
It is not a good sign to feel like you are
characters in a Carver short story, imprisoned
between exposition and denouement. It is
not a good sign that you lift your good ear from
the pillow to listen with envy to the cats screeching and yowling
in the wrestling bout that passes for kitty lovemaking.
And, if you think of David Hume, formulating
some theory of human rationality in an ivy-covered
brownstone, that is, trust me, not a good sign either.
Okay, we are all wondering when we will achieve
the sort of ambulatory deathhood our
parents called "maturity." Okay, we all
want to stop longing for Milk Duds as we're
funnelled toward the register. Okay.
Okay, okay, okay. But the bed is unmade;
the refrigerator chokes on the rot-slick arugula.
Flies attend the rebirth of the onions,
the bananas whose steep trajectory toward
inedibility can be frightening. Especially
at 3 am. Especially when your face in the
fluorescent mirror is beginning to achieve
the geological splendor of W. H. Auden's. In
his late years. In the days of erudition and settled
decadence. In the days of cucumber salads

and smoking jackets. In the days of. In
the days. But, let's face it: You don't
know jack about Auden. But you do know
The Monkees' theme song and that you
insist on singing it in the mornings, over coffee,
in the shower, while shaving, may explain
your wife's troubled sleep. And what else do
you know? The names of several breeds of dogs
(Shelty, Blue Heeler, Ridgeback, Basenji); how
to make a tolerable pitcher of Kool Aid; that
the phrase "Do No Harm" may be a basic tenet
of one of the world's major religions; that Pete
Maravich's nickname was "Pistol," that Walter
Williams' was "No Neck"; that Jesus Christ
had twelve disciples or apostles; that dragging
your disc icon to the trash will not cause
your disc to be trashed; that Paul Westerberg,
once a self-loathing jerk who wrote and sang
some killer rock 'n' roll, now has "matured"
into a kind of ambulatory deathhood that augurs well
for his financial and physical health; that "mutually
assured destruction" was, at one time,
considered a bad thing. Of course, you cannot
stop yourself from thinking if this poem
were only a sonnet, a villanelle, if this poem were
in rhymed quatrains, heroic couplets, if this poem
were read over a smoky saxophone solo, if this poem
had shipped platinum, if this poem were in celebration
of some waffling politician's inauguration.
But you tell yourself: If just one person. If just one
person accidentally stumbles across this poem
and is moved. Say in a used book store. In San Francisco.
And he walks out of the store chuckling softly
to himself. Above him, through the wash of streetlights

he notices the stars. Strangers walking down the sidewalks
seem part of some great, benign, and mildly humorous
plan. He begins to see relationships between the
random motions of vehicles and the way language
developed in the human species. The future
seems surprisingly coherent, riddled with possibilities, like,
like maggots in road kill, he thinks. And, blinded by
the brilliance of your language, he wanders into traffic.
Miraculously, cars, trolleys, buses somehow avoid
squashing him. He's become a cartoon character.
Like Mr. Magoo. Blind, carefree, incapable of surviving.
A liability. An economic disaster. A poet. He short-cuts
through a construction site. A wrecking ball knocks off his cap;
a cinder block falls eight stories and smashes at his feet.
He makes it to his apartment. He climbs the stairs.
There's a note on the door. I can't take it anymore,
the note says. It's pinned to the door with a meat cleaver.
Resonant image, he thinks. He enters the apartment—
pants over a chair back, books scattered on the floor—
regarding it all with his newfound aesthetic distance.
Balled-up socks like river rocks. Mop head
like an octopus in the sink.

» "Untitled, 1985," by Agnes Martin: A Misreading

Not nothing, though close to it.
Nor wood, exactly, though wood
Is evoked (but evocation is not

The point). The knots not knots.
Exactitude, not rectitude.
(That connection severed.) Nothingness

Measured & partitioned. Severed
First from the exacting hand,
Since act is not & also is the point.

The actor finds her mark & stands
On nonexistent boards, exactly
As the script requires. A severity

Scripted, yet also unscripted—eight
Boards, also not boards, as
Ink & watercolor find their—But wait:

She's inked these wooden blinds
Shut. These blinds not blinds, instead
Are *yet & also, but & though.*

In Nonquitt where the wooden shingles weather,
The troubled children pluck guitars and, dreamy
In the shade of pines, sing "Mom is getting better."

Though Dad is long and longer between letters,
The curtains close so everything seems seemly
In Nonquitt where the wooden shingles weather.

Brother Nathan throws a frisbee to the setter.
A dose of prozac makes him smile and, beaming
In the shade of pines, sing "Mom is getting better."

Sister Kate grows thick beneath her sweater,
And the youngest, Kip, has wrecked her mom's new Beamer,
In Nonquitt where the wooden shingles weather.

Mom just sobs and sleeps in late and later,
While Nate and Kate and Kip are just a dream
In the shade of pines singing "Mom is getting better."

But when the check arrives on Monday, everyone together—
Minus Dad who is shacked-up with his dreamgirl—
In Nonquitt where the wooden shingles weather,
In the shade of pines, sings "Mom is getting better."

» The Gropingest Grope of All Gropers

Was a gringo, a gamer, a guppy-lush geegaw,
who stole in the night to the wine bar askew.

His hat was all flimflam, his mouth half-aghast,
awash in st-stammer and thrust. His parry,

a party, a partly-posh soiree, a glimpse and a gush
and a slap on the butt. His hands wandered wary

for wary was he, that tentacled tit-monger and
kisser to boot. Brute boot, to be sure, hallowed

and hollowed and power-mad, too. Who adores
a fascist abhors a boor. His lingua was franca,

his linguine, al dente, and paired with vin gris,
for the gropingest grope of all gropers was he.

Now that your work has come to nothing
And the planet, too, is lost;
The prestigious prizes grifted,
And the stones of greatness mossed;

Now that land is storm-tossed, quaked,
The seas a tangle of plastic;
And poets are given to hue and cry,
More icon than iconoclastic;

Now that the faces are selling the books,
And fame has abducted the muse;
Let's rage, rage against the death of the light,
Then, truculent, turn to the booze.

» Letter to M.

Those troglodytes you ravished in the Tuillerie were never
among my favorites. I had hoped you would avenge yourself
with the pallid stockbroker who crimped my Pinto. Such
callousness notwithstanding, I long still
for the incandescence of your linguistic events.
As for my nights, I spend them tooling along the plangent
Avenida de Shitkickers here in El Paso, where the jackrabbits'
incessant leaping and twitching reminds me of the
by-now-famous "interpretive dance"
you performed at Tommy's Show Club. Though what
you were interpreting and for whom remains obscure,
I don't begrudge you the peso-filled waistband or
the festival of macho posturing that ensued. I do, however,
wish that you'd assigned me a more suitable role.
While appearing as a Minister of God satisfied some
deep craving for a more virtuous existence, it placed me
in a somewhat compromised position vis-à-vis those cretins
who pursued you to the jukebox and then alternately
cackled and swooned outside your dressing room door.
You will recall you thought they were "sweet"
until they hurled a dwarf over the partition. Might
I suggest that you also misjudged me? You questioned
my intentions. Fair enough. By now, it should be clear
that your breasts were part of the attraction, as were
your characteristic, if somewhat obtuse, syntactical procedures.
Frankly, I never minded being called "Ralphie," and your
refusal to recognize me on the street caused only a tremor
of chagrin. If you will meet me outside the Three Star
Desert Motel, I will return your pet nematodes, and perhaps
we can share a Coruscating Camisole in the lobby bar.
Remember how we used to set them aflame

with your "Bugling Elk" lighter? I shall never forget
the first time you raised your face from the fuming chalice—
your singed eyebrows, your necklace of fire. If you will wear
your velvet jodhpurs, I will wear my loin cloth
and fashion my hair into the Evil Knievel upsweep,
whose meaning remains obscure, rooted as you always said,
in our age's "profound cultural myopia."

» The Rejected

We have read your work and found it lacking. But lacking what? A certain *joie de vivre*, a peculiar and icy *fond du lac*? A Tutankhamun of the spirit? A spriteliness? Is it the marked lack of pratfalls? An embolus of dirges rising through the femoral? Who taped these phalanges under the dashboard, strapped the terriers to the luggage rack? Surely your prosody should alleviate such suffering? Or elide it? Or pass over it in silence or something (a vague muttering from the next room, a muffled yipping from the *llano*, a drunken chanting in the borstal) approximating silence. Please keep us in mind with new work. Perhaps something more like your "Vegetal Sonnets" or "Precambrian Odes: A Sequence," which we found initially promising, but whose opportunities seemed often squandered by your choice of form. We want to support your emanations, if only they weren't so ephemeral, if only your *cri de coeur* weren't so lacking in *coeur.*

Election, *n.* A contest of wills between those who won't.

*

A conservative has bad intentions; a liberal thinks having good
    intentions is enough.

*

The rumors are wrong. I'm actually quite sufferable.

*

Poetry, *n.* A narrowing of the prose for which there is no known cure.

*

No good ever comes of a diorama.

*

Politics, *n.* a skirmish of opportunism masquerading as a cavalcade of
    hopes.

*

New study reveals there will never be enough studies.

*

In America, everybody loves poets. They just don't want them getting
    into the house.

*

Writing prose poems is like playing tennis without a ball.

*

Speaking truth to power is like reading Wittgenstein to a dachshund.

*

Religious Studies: The skinny monk / makes of thinness a virtue.

*

Wild poetry is often ignored because it can't be saddled up and ridden
    in the fenced arena of the essay.

*

Poetry doesn't explain the world; it rescues the world from explanation.

*

I'm at two with nature.

*

Poets experience life more deeply than the rest of us—and then make
us feel bad by writing about it.

*

Publication is not proof of excellence, it's evidence of persistence.

*

Poetry is to fiction as a kleptomaniac is to baking.

*

Relax, poets. *Crazy* is in the job description.

*

Activist/Poet, *n.* Activist.

*

Deconstruction, *n.* The art of dismantling someone else's text and using
the materials of that text to construct a far superior text of your
own while maintaining that nothing can be built of anything.

*

Never pay a poet by the hour.

*

Why does the age at which you finally know how to write coincide so
perfectly with the age at which you have nothing to say?

*

I'm working on my groundbreaking book, *The Fetishization of
Fetishization*.

*

Procrastination is a kind of poetry.

*

Artistic elitist, *n.* Someone who tries to do something well, thereby
oppressing those who would rather not.

*

I'm writing for the ages. It'd be good if we had some.

Gone, the quiet of toads. We used to see them
half-buried in the powdery dirt. I liked their eyes,
the nictating membrane. They seemed wry, a little smug.
Like a girl who is double-jointed. Demonstrating that. At recess.

Gone the articles, how they coddled their nouns.
Or, sometimes, volunteered them. Did I mention
the car crash? That gone, too. Did I mention
the lost reveries of childhood? *A career, you say? Built on those?*

How strange. Must have been a slight career. There was a bittern
in a white pine. I got so close. Held an owl on my finger
under a sky of crows. The subtext kept leaching into the text.
In therapy, they would call it "Fear of Abandonment."

You could almost hear the capital letters. There should have been
a twelve-step program for the cats, hissing and swatting each other
on the lawn: *I mated with your mother. I ate the mouse you were toying with
(and which you were probably saving for dinner). I lapped up the milk*

*your owner intended for you. I acknowledged a higher power,
but there seemed to be a mechanism somewhere inside and—
bad news—it wasn't a brain.* The good news—I read it this morning—
is that the male mantis gets to keep his head. I mean that literally.

Would that we were so lucky. I mean that figuratively.
A career, you say? The female mantises in the experiments were probably
just hungry, underfed. And the head is an excellent snack.
Except that the eyes and mouth are attached,

one can imagine a cat getting through his day without one.
A horse, however, is a different story. Not that there's much
of importance there—just the source of a horse's errors.
Like mistaking the wind for a predator or mistaking

the glint off a shard of glass for a predator or mistaking
a cedar tree for a predator or mistaking a rubber ball
for a predator or mistaking a predator for a barn door.
And what is a horse but a choir of misprisions? Isn't that why

we love to guide them? Isn't that why they need us so?
But I was talking about childhood. Lost reveries. "Fear of Abandonment."
Listen, you can almost hear the car starting, the clutch pedal's
thump, the heart beating its fists inside the four-year-old's chest.

» Final Exam

Were you standing near that mud-heavy river where the mergansers
 twitched and plunged?

Did you turn in the caul of it in the open of it looking everywhere?

Were you breathing deeply the chaff-inflected air?

Did you see the sun where it grazed the hilltop?

Feel the wet air the still pocket of heat you huddled inside?

Hear thin gurglings where the river swirled along the bank?

Did you see the willow? Black mud? Bees?

Pink wild roses scattered in the brush?

Were you waiting for someone?

Did it all matter? Did it mean something?

Say what it meant.

I thank the editors of the following journals for publishing these poems, some in earlier versions:

"Beauty," *Taos Journal of International Poetry & Art*

"Of Gwendolyn Brooks," *Golden Shovel Anthology*, Fayetteville, AR: University of Arkansas Press, 2016

"In History," *Thelonious Sphere,* Lubbock, TX: Q Ave. Press, 2013

"Henry at 70. Dawn. Tulum." *Heteronymy: An Anthology*, Nacogdoches, TX: LaNana Creek Press, 2015

"Passing," *Terrain.org*

"Monk Plays Stride," *Thelonious Sphere,* Lubbock, TX: Q Ave. Press, 2013

"The Failed Spring," *Terrain.org*

"Memorandum: Inputting Outcomes Assessments for Individuals Currently Enrolled as Post-Secondary Arts Consumers: A Report Composed by the Consulting Group Upon Completion of the Recent Site Visit," *Platte Valley Review*

"After Conducting a Thorough but Preliminary Investigation," *Obsidian II*

"Blue Monk," *Thelonious Sphere,* Lubbock, TX: Q Ave. Press, 2013

"Apocalypse," *The Laurel Review*

"Henry at 70. His Skittish Rut." *Heteronymy: An Anthology*, Nacogdoches, TX: LaNana Creek Press, 2015

"The Campaign Manager Talks Shop," *Ontario Review* and in *Local Color*, Aiken, SC: Palanquin Press, 1995

"Letter to Rob from Bear Creek," *Poetry at Sangam* (India)

"The Rebel Makes His Stand Before Leaving," *Ontario Review* and in *Local Color*, Aiken, SC: Palanquin Press, 1995

"Leadbelly," *Countermeasures*

"Bucky Sherman's Letter to the God of Winds," *turnrow*

"Bucky Sherman's Letter to the God of Covenants," *turnrow*

"Maturity," *Indiana Review*

"'Untitled, 1985,' by Agnes Martin: A Misreading," *Ekphrastic.*

"In Nonquitt Where the Wooden Shingles Weather," *Countermeasures*

"The Gropingest Grope of all Gropers, *The Telepoem Booth*

"Letter to M," *Exquisite Corpse*

"The Rejected," *The Laurel Review*

"From *The Notebooks of Chuck Calabreze*," *Sonder*

"A Choir of Misprisions," *Ploughshares*

The epigraph from Nicanor Parra's "Recuerdos de juventud" was translated by W.S. Merwin.

With thanks to the Lannan Foundation, the Artists' Retreat at Cill Rialaig, and the Institute of American Indian Arts for the gift of time; to Greg Glazner, Dana Levin, and Arthur Sze for looking at early drafts of this book; to Teresa, for her support and for understanding when I needed to disappear into the keyboard or notebook to chase an ephemeral poem; and to Elizabeth Murphy for getting this unkempt manuscript a nice suit and some new shoes.

NOTE: Several of the poems in this book were written in a form I invented that I call "Trading Fours," based on the group improvisation technique used by jazz musicians in which each musician takes a brief, four-bar solo. I originally conceived of it as a collaborative form with each poet writing four lines based on the previous poet's quatrain. Often, I would begin, as in jazz improvisation, with a "head." In jazz, the head would usually be a well-known melody. In poetry, it might be, say, four lines from Sylvia Plath. Each successive poet was required to repeat words either from the "head" (if they were the first poet to "solo") or the previous poet's quatrain, preferably in a different form (a noun could become an adjective, adverb, or verb; a verb could become a noun, adjective, or adverb). A homonym also could be substituted. The pattern for repetition is ABCD DCBA. I think the form proved too tedious for my potential collaborators, so I began trading fours with myself.

JON DAVIS is the author of five poetry chapbooks and five previous full-length collections of poetry: *Improbable Creatures, Heteronymy: An Anthology, Preliminary Report, Scrimmage of Appetite,* and *Dangerous Amusements.* He was co-translator, with the author, of Iraqi poet Naseer Hassan's *Dayplaces.* Davis has received a Lannan Literary Award in Poetry, the Peter I.B. Lavan Prize from the Academy of American Poets, the Off the Grid Poetry Prize, and two National Endowment for the Arts' poetry fellowships. He was the city of Santa Fe's fourth Poet Laureate and taught for 23 years at the Institute of American Indian Arts before founding, in 2013, the IAIA low residency MFA in Creative Writing, which he directed until his retirement in 2018.